Frost Flowers

New Women's Voices Series, No. 147

poems by

Winifred Hughes

Finishing Line Press
Georgetown, Kentucky

Frost Flowers

New Women's Voices Series, No. 147

ACKNOWLEDGMENTS

Ars Interpres: "As Close"
Asheville Review: "Intervals"
Snowy Egret: "Banding Station"
U.S. 1 Worksheets: "A Parting"

It is a great pleasure to acknowledge the many years of support and critique so
unstintingly provided by members of U.S. 1 Poets Cooperative and Princeton
Research Forum—you know who you are. It has been a privilege to participate
in the numerous poetry events sponsored by the D&R Greenway Land Trust
under the leadership of Linda Mead and Carolyn Edelmann. Special thanks
are due to the rump poetry group of Emily Nguyen, Shelley Kiernan, and
Judith McNally, and to the regulars at Emily's Long Poems Gatherings,
including Frederick Tibbetts, Lois Marie Harrod, Elizabeth Socolow, and
David Herrstrom. My sister, Hildred Crill, and my late mother, Josephine
Nicholls Hughes, are my poetic models, *le migliori fabbre*. My husband, Fred
Spar, and our sons, Adam and Alex, have variously encouraged, objected to,
and put up with both of my addictions—to birding and to poetry.

Publisher: Leah Maines
Editor: Christen Kincaid
Cover Art and Design: Liam Crill
Author Photo: Adam Spar

Printed in the USA on acid-free paper.
Order online: www.finishinglinepress.com
         also available on amazon.com

Author inquiries and mail orders:
Finishing Line Press
P. O. Box 1626
Georgetown, Kentucky 40324
U. S. A.

Table of Contents

To Fred always

LOOKING FOR THE FLOWER

Looking for the flower, I found
    the bud, furtive among leaves,
        self wrapped around self;

looking for the flower, pulled the bud
    to hard green pieces before unfolding
        the sticky mysteries;

looking for the flower of the flower,
    tore off petals, *loves, loves
        not,* caught by the binary;

looking for the flower in the seedpod,
    spilled out unnumbered centers,
        scattered the flower to the wind.

A PARTING

Stony Brook: water rushing over stubborn
      rocks, jagged outcrops, bare feet

scraped, stumbling upstream against
      the current, against the past tumbling

all around me, the stream where we walked
      together, after you told me and I

could hardly take it in, could hardly feel
      the stones, the clear cold water

shattering, numbing my bare skin, the way
      stony, our words too like stones.

WHITE SNAKEROOT

There it is in our backyard: innocent haze
of inflorescence, unfocused, slightly formless

like a distracted cloud among scraggly foliage,
inserting itself unasked for. Early settlers

made tea from its bitter rhizomes to treat fever
or kidney stones, poultices for snakebite.

I had no idea it could be so toxic, causing
"milk sickness" if cows ingested it in the field.

Lincoln's mother died of it. Think of the energy
it puts into trying to poison us, while we harbor it

unknowingly, the delicate florets with stamens groping
like tiny hooks, last of the wildflowers to bloom in fall.

BITTERN

Sometimes it can be hard to tell
        the bittern from the marsh; rushes,
phragmites, cattails and the shadows
        on them from the streaky long neck,

bill tilted upward, stilt-like legs. The bittern
        can stand rigid, pointing at the sky,
an hour or more, out in the open, not
        thinking it can be seen but melting

into the marsh, becoming one with it. Hard
        to tell its stillness from the marsh's
stillness, its silence from the marsh's thrum.
        One day in April it will appear, stealthy,

centered, utterly itself; after much reflection,
        it will spear a frog. When it will vanish
again, who can tell? A thought, forsaking
        the mind, but not without a trace.

SPRING FROST

Raw spring torn from
winter by ragged handfuls,

stark light, bare bones
of trees stripped to the quick,

scabbed with hard-clenched
buds. Fallow earth is turned

over by the blade in keening
wind, air throbbing with

the flicker's whirring cry,
its ringing tattoo. First

flowers almost in bloom,
browning with the frost.

VEERY/VIREO

Deep in the greening canopy, playing
        hide but don't seek, a small bird sings

incessantly, unstintingly: *Here I am.*
        Vireo. Conjugates it: To be green,

I too am green. To flourish in spring.
        To be fresh as leafbud, verdant shoots

of grasses, unfurling ferns. To have been
        unrealized. To be here. Simply be.

And the veery's ethereal scales descend:
        Veer-u, veer-u, veer, veer, dispersing

their particles of sound into the fabric
        of things, swerving the woods to song.

INTERVALS

How does the apple blossom know
to shape itself within a perfect pentagram,
unfurl blank petals only and always

numbering five, pull apart from the bud
in more directions than the compass allows,
leave the apple to bear a five-pointed star

at its heart. And the daisy opening its eye
unfolds the florets in logarithmic lines
that intersect one another, clockwise

and counter, beading slowly into seed
along the measured intervals of song.
Galaxies unwind from a single node

as our bodies radiate, center to verge:
this is the shape of the world, coiled
helix, blown petals on the grass.

MOMENTARILY

If it goes unrecorded, will the moment be
lost or more itself? Will it slip through

the interstices, fade into the next as it
absorbed the one before? Just a moment—

will it be longer or shorter, will we be in it
or oblivious, will it still unite us in time

if not in place or in temper, will it last
exactly for a moment and no more

but equally no less? Is it in this spill
of sunlight over newly green willows,

in the glance of water over stones? In this one
afternoon of nothing more? Of such stillness

melting into itself and into itself until we can't
tell but think maybe, and then it is gone.

AN ABSENCE

Under the arched bridge by the old mill,
the rough-winged swallows were flooded out

of their hollowed nests, after a spring storm
that swelled the water in the abandoned mill race,

swamped the spillway, wedged a tree trunk
whole against the stone headwall. The swallows

skittered about aimlessly in the heavy air, uttering
their harsh, burry cries. They could not settle

on the wires or the slim branches to roost or preen.
They could not settle. Within days, they had flown,

and the skies over the bridge and the mill race were empty
of their pointed wings and wide-hinged bills. Their young

will not fledge here this year, will not gather in restless
flocks, will not return where they have never been.

IN THE MIDST

Fall blackbirds by the hundreds
                by the tens of hundreds
                                converge overhead
            in their loose formations

                                flexible skeins
                    netting the skies
            from all directions
                                doubling back
                    through themselves

                in a sinuous coil
porous geodesic dome
                            of motion and sound
                                inelegant squawks
                                        lost
                in indistinguishable din

uproar as of feathered engines
                when they lift
                        on sudden pulse
                            from the field

                        each in its own
                pocket of air
                                suspended
    on the updraft
                    at equidistant angles
                            from the others
                        submerged
                            into the whole

               overflowing
        as one indestructible
                          entity
        one instinct
                honed

                not euphonious
        but euphoric
                          irresistibly
                                    alive.

ARBOREAL

Trees go slowly, take their time unfolding,
a century or so as saplings, making do

with the filtered light that drifts down from
the canopy, stretching tentative filaments

under the leafmoldy soil, laying up layers
of dense woody fiber, nodule by nodule,

ring by annual ring—frugal, unobtrusive,
thinking nothing of waiting their turn to break

through to the sun, spend four or five hundred years
in basking, expanding their manifold green canvases

under blistering rays. Gropingly, their roots will meet,
entangle, pass on messages or nutrients to a whole

community. If one staggers or quails, its comrades
will shoulder its weight; if it falls, they will nourish

its stump, further extending the long slow length
of its time in the living forest. We try to hurry the trees,

force them to grow spindly trunks at unnatural speed,
harvest prematurely, replant in rows. We have no

patience for them, for their almost imperceptible
rhythms, in our haste to be born and buried.

BANDING CATBIRDS
(for H.S.)

She holds the soft grey feathers
against my ear—warm, struggling,

the heart so small, so whole, so quick
it fills my own with faster beating,

so loud it cancels hearing, and I feel
nothing else, so close now to the wild

heart of living so intensely it is almost
death, so few ounces of sinew coiled

to explode from her straining fingers.
But first the mist net, sky itself

entangling, frenzied wings beating
against the frenzied heart, plunge into

the dark bag, the scale, the calipers, the metal
band clamped around the reed-thin leg,

weight it will carry with it; first the bird
in her hand, as she gently fans out

a plicate wing, strokes a stray feather
into place, before the sudden shock

of release. It's only a catbird back
in the sky, in the underbrush, in its secret

life, just where she wants it, banded
but still unchanged, beyond her reach.

AT THE JETTIES

Stone chimneys loosely piled
above the dunes—all that remains

of a phantom house, and I think,
this is the past, what it looks like

now. I think, *I have lived*
in this house. I've tasted

the salt air, looked out through
exactly this angle of light

onto this grey sea, I remember
the shape of the waves, that's what

memory is, the shape of waves,
and when the waves recede

strange shapes of driftwood, sea
wrack, sea glass, grey smoke

wavering from stone chimneys,
after flames had engulfed the house.

CRATER

It startles every time I round
the corner from marsh to woods—

a silver beech, its slender trunk
bashed in, the shape and height

of a man, top hat and squared shoulders,
deeply gouged as though the man himself

had rushed headlong against the tree,
blundered into it, into the black

cavity at its heart, some unimaginable
depth, inhuman but not inadequate

to take him in. I suppose he never
reappeared. I wonder how the beech

survived—a thin sliver of live bark
to hold it upright all these years around

the man-shaped crater. I was told
it had been struck by lightening,

but that I could never quite believe.

BANDING STATION

Thin-skinned: it lends new meaning
to the word. Hold a passerine face up,

gently blow away the feathers
from its breast, look right through

the epidermis: you can see entrails,
the dark liver, a robin's chest

bursting with its heart that's beating
so much faster than your own.

In fall, before migration, visible
pads of fat; in breeding season,

the brood patch—bare skin, blood
vessels crowding the surface to form

a vascular edema, the robin's swollen
body creating heat to warm the eggs.

Measure quickly, release the calipers:
the bird can't tell you from a sharp-shinned

hawk toying with its prey. Leave a metal
band clamped around one leg.

UNDER THE CANOPY

A tanager is singing in the canopy
its raspy, full-hearted song, note after

note descending, wafting down through
the pollen-heavy air to the forest floor

where I am standing rooted, enthralled,
scanning for the bright scarlet bird and not

stealing a glimpse of it—so vivid, so
inaccessible in its unseen world,

moving as a thought through my mind
as I walk through the woods, interloper

in this space with my overwrought notions
of what cannot be known, only guessed,

of what is hidden from us, yet apprehended,
like a tanager in the canopy.

CHAPPAQUIDDICK BLUES

Edgy, precipitous—who builds
          a mansion on a cliff top
where the coastline ebbs
          and flows erratically,
                    who dares the raw
                              Atlantic
          to start its gnawing and licking,
                    contentious riptides
                              undermining
                    the basic premises
          on which his argument
                              is foundering?

And when the bluff recedes,
                              ungrounds
                    stability,
          who will hoist up his house
                    on trestles and dollies
          and creep inland
                    snail-like
                              by inches,
afraid to front the elements,
                    to pitch the construct
          of his intent
                              headlong
                    over the brink?

SMALL-LEAF RHODODENDRON IN DECEMBER

Among round blackened leaves, black buds
        swollen with longing, with impatience,
split themselves open into pale purplish finery,
        seduced by one warm afternoon, out

of all season, defiant of December, to give
        away what they cannot take back—
soft furls of flesh with their frail, complex
        sex organs, set trembling in a wind

that will soon turn northerly, ice-bearing
        air that will stiffen petals, halt
the half-blown blooms, leave the small bush
        in a frieze of unavailing desire.

THE TERNS AT KATAMA

Above the bay's surface terns
            on sleek skittering wings
        hover and
plunge
        not in unison but
                changing places
        weaving in
                and out
                        of other wings.

They are not thinking of
        pattern
                of syncopation
        they are not
thinking
        each plunge a mouthful
                of silversides glinting
        in water writhing
through burning air.

More often than not
        they come up
                empty
                        unsatisfied
harsh cries
        reverberating
                white wings flailing
        plunge and
plunge again.

OUR BOX ELDER TREE

Swamp maple—unrecruited volunteer,
weed tree sending out shoots and suckers

blindly, shapelessly, from its stand
in boggy bottomland, careless of wet feet

or uncertain ground, not long-lived
but urgent, even reckless in its time.

This particular tree is in decline, nearing
the end of its span, great limbs dying back,

stripped of bark, yet still held aloft like
arms in supplication—or is it joy, sheer

stubbornness and will? In autumn, literally
seedy, it hatches swarms of red-and-black

beetles—box elder bugs—harmless, useless,
but annoyingly redundant, directionless,

blundering about. In winter and spring,
it harbors woodpeckers that girdle

the living trunk for sap, excavate nest
cavities in the decaying pulp. We hesitate

to chop it down, to lose its habitat, its brio,
its precarious refusal to fall.

AS CLOSE

We are drawn to the floating world, to its frank reversals:
this whole November morning pitched headlong. Trees bare

or burnished, doubly rooted, grip appositional skies, fallen
branches a closed circle, while a spent leaf plunges into

itself, drifts there suspended. A heron, hunched motionless,
is reflecting on another, wavering; a pointed rooftop hoists

the oblong of its building. We peer at the sun's silvery coin
tossed in carelessly, that other world a wish attached to this one.

And the narrow channel deep enough to hold it all, our alternate
lives waiting there submerged, as close as slipping in.

FOXY

At dusk on a suburban street, though rarely,
it might materialize against the blacktop,
potholes, low pickets on a fence: a red fox,
bringing with it a pause, a tense stillness,

aura of something otherworldly, a depth
into which everything might vanish.
The fox moves fluidly, tail a stiff conical
brush held slightly away from its body,

eyes an unwinking stare, whether taking us in
or repelling the sight of us we can't quite
tell. Are we wilding, going feral, overgrown
with weeds like an abandoned lot, or is it

gentrifying, reaching an accommodation
with its near-destroyer, with the universal
predator that paved over its secret pathways.
Why are we the ones who feel afraid?

THE ROSE-BREASTED GROSBEAK'S NEST

A few sticks carelessly assembled
in the low crook of a weedy bush
set swaying by every accidental gust
where the female grosbeak, stick-colored, dissembles

before changing places with the male, which presses
hard against the sticks with its wounded-looking breast,
shows off, unheedingly, that gaudy signal of distress.
The hatchlings, stick figures attached to clumps of downy fluff,

gape and swallow, regardless of the breeze that trembles
through their airy nursery; they're used to flux,
they ride it out, not knowing it resembles

their own slight hold on lives that may be tossed
at any moment to the ground, among the brambles
from which untested wings might flush.

SPRING MIGRANTS

Against what odds, after what journeying,
this single Yellow-throated Warbler,
wearing its few ounces of feather

and flesh, has arrived exactly here—
in this tangle of spicebush—exactly
now—at the moment I reach the same

spot on the path along this April stream
where the spicebush unlocks its tentative,
yellow-green blossoms, the color of leaves.

How did I get here, over what irrecoverable
distances, so close to home, so far
from my setting out?—following what

irrefutable instinct, or was it stumbling
randomly, foolishly, without the migrant's
unquestioning compass? Should I have been

somewhere else when he alighted and broke
into song—the slow, intricate, downslurred
syllables uttered at leisurely intervals.

Or is this where I was headed all along,
to this brief encounter, this moment as full
as any, as much as I can manage to take in?

HARRY'S BROOK IS SINGING

In the quiet dark, we listen for it
—inaudible by day, now softly
muttering, tumbling into itself

over heaped-up stones, teasing
logjams into song—what we meant
to say but forgot or were afraid of

saying, our words jumbled and jangled
in the brook's stuttering flow. No looking
back, we see that, no need to repeat

its watery parables, no belated apology
or alibis. We stand on the porch
together and listen, clasping hands.

FROST FLOWERS

Too late for the other kind—fleshy
       petals, flashy colors, turgid
pistil and stamen—frostweed makes
       do with what it has, pulling

water from ground not quite frozen
       into stems cracked by the cold,
extruding slithers of ice, unfurling
       ribbons and whorls of it,

white or transparent, that blossom
       overnight into spun sugar,
only to dissolve in sun. If you try
       to pick them, they will shatter.

Shall I offer them to you, because it's
       autumn where we find ourselves,
because we know what is beautiful,
       what will vanish at our touch?

Raised in an academic family, **Winifred Hughes** started out as an academic herself, earning a Ph.D. in English literature at Brown University and teaching in the English department at Princeton University. Her scholarly book, *The Maniac in the Cellar: Sensation Novels of the 1860s*, was published by Princeton University Press.

She is married to Fred Spar, Chinese historian and business consultant; they have two grown sons, Adam and Alex. When her children were small, she found that she no longer had the time or attention span for three-volume Victorian novels, her previous field of research; gradually she began reading and writing lyric poems instead. Over the years since, her poems have appeared in *Poetry, Poetry Northwest, Atlanta Review, The Literary Review, International Poetry Review,* and *Appalachia,* among other journals. "Dyslexic" has been recorded for the Poetry Foundation's permanent audio archive. "Kingfishers Catch Fire" won the 2014 Wild Leaf Press poetry award. Her chapbook, *Nine-Bend Bridge,* won the 2015 Red Berry Editions summer chapbook competition. She has been the recipient of two independent artist fellowships from the New Jersey State Council on the Arts. She is a longtime member of U.S. 1 Poets Cooperative and Princeton Research Forum.

All along, she has remained an active hiker and birder, spending as much time as possible outdoors. Currently she leads bird walks in the local wildlife refuge and teaches a course in literature and nature at the Watershed Institute in Pennington, NJ.

The poems in *Frost Flowers* bring together her two lifelong passions, coming as they do from the place of interface between language and direct experience of the natural world. She has always been fascinated by form, in nature and in poetry: as a flower or leaf unfolds, so a poem takes shape in sound, rhythm, line, and stanza. Human language is itself a natural phenomenon, not separating us from other species and our shared environment but ideally connecting us, bringing us closer. She has always tried to be mindful of Thoreau's vision of the poet as transplanting words to the page "with earth adhering to their roots." Writing about nature has taken on increasing urgency, as the wild places of the planet are increasingly despoiled; it has become nothing less than a matter of bearing witness to what is being lost and what remains.

www.ingramcontent.com/pod-product-compliance
Lightning Source LLC
LaVergne TN
LVHW051612080426
835510LV00020B/3251